GOLF COURSE MATH AND SPRAY CALIBRATIONS

Also included Safe chemical handling

GENERAL MATH AND BUDGET MATH FOR GOLF COURSE SUPERINTENDENTS, ASSISTANT SUPERINTENDENTS AND EVERYONE ELSE

By

Eugene Weiser
Superintendent
The Meadows Golf Course
Litchfield, ME

SO, WHAT IS GOLF COURSE MATH

Golf math is generally addition, subtraction division, and multiplication. Everything you learned throughout your school days. We find some algebra and geometry that helps us find area and square footage. Many ask what the big deal is and it's a very simple explanation. You assistants and spray techs need to know how much your putting down and remain compliant with state laws. It is also included on many state pesticide applicator tests.

Irrigation techs need to know what percentages of water is being used and amounts being placed in certain areas. You will need to know how much water is being drained from irrigation sources, especially if the greens committees or local environmental groups ask for specifics.

Budget math is similar, especially if you need to know time allowances for budgeting, equipment usage and repair times, down times, and expenditures. It's also helpful to know budgeting basics to see where expenses are overriding savings to adjust for the year and future planning.

Throughout this book I will include samples and screen shots to make it easier to understand. Along with the basic, I will also include simplified math to make this easier to understand. I will include labels from pesticides and then show calculations for specific areas that are generally found on golf courses such as figuring out 2 or

3 acres of green coverage for a specific application rate. The appendix will include general tables for most problems found.

While much of what you see will be found throughout the internet as everything is these days, I want to simplify everything in an easy to understand format and apply many years' of my experience into one book for the up and coming.

The best place to start the fun is with sprayer calibrations simply because it figures into your application calibrations. Yes, many new sprayers are equipped with computers that do the figuring for you, jut punch and go. The problem with that is you are depending on the computer to be right all the time or like many of us old timers, you have an old Toro Multi-pro 1100 with the pro control spray system. Yep, they are still out there and work just fine (if you have a good mechanic, low budget, and maintain it yearly). These require the old method of calculations.

SPRAYER NOZZELS FOR CALCULATIONS

Nozzles are the most important part of your calibrations, provided everything is running properly. Calibrations should be performed before the start of the season, at least twice per season and any time you change nozzles. Every nozzle has a different flow rate and switching will change your application rate, sometimes substantially.

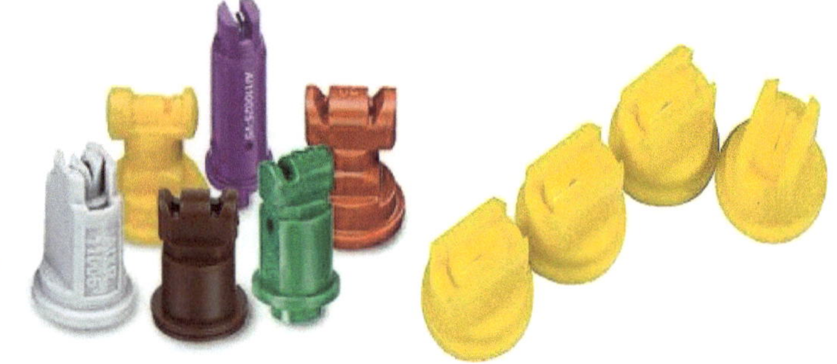

Figure 1 Air injection Nozzle   **Figure 2 Typical Yellow standard nozzle**

Figures 1 and 2 show typical nozzles uses on your boom sprayer, though Tee-Jet has many more with exact specifications for each one. These are found online in their catalog, to aid in calibrating your sprayer.

Nozzle Size*	Orifice Dia.(In.)	40 PSI	100 PSI	250 PSI	500 PSI	600 PSI	700 PSI	800 PSI	1000 PSI	1200 PSI	1500 PSI	2000 PSI	2500 PSI	3000 PSI	3500 PSI	4000 PSI	5000 PSI	6000 PSI	7000 PSI
2	.034	.20	.32	.50	.71	.77	.80	.89	1.0	1.1	1.2	1.4	1.6	1.7	1.9	2.0	2.24	?	?
4	.052	.40	.63	1.00	1.40	1.60	1.70	1.80	2.0	2.2	2.5	2.8	3.1	3.5	3.8	4.0	4.5	4.9	5.3
4.5	.055	.45	.71	1.10	1.50	1.70	1.90	2.00	2.2	2.4	2.8	3.0	3.6	3.9	4.3	4.5	5.0	5.5	5.9
5	.057	.50	.79	1.30	1.80	1.90	2.10	2.20	2.5	2.8	3.1	3.6	4.0	4.4	4.7	5.0	5.6	6.1	6.6
5.5	.060	.55	.87	1.40	1.90	2.10	2.30	2.50	2.8	3.0	3.4	3.8	4.4	4.8	5.2	5.5	6.2	6.7	7.3
6	.062	.60	.95	1.50	2.10	2.30	2.50	2.70	3.0	3.2	3.7	4.2	4.8	5.2	5.6	6.0	6.7	7.3	7.9
6.5	.064	.65	1.00	1.70	2.30	2.50	2.70	2.90	3.3	3.6	4.0	4.6	5.2	5.7	6.0	6.5	7.3	8.0	8.6
7	.067	.70	1.10	1.80	2.50	2.70	2.90	3.10	3.5	3.8	4.3	5.0	5.6	6.1	6.6	7.0	7.8	8.6	9.3
7.5	.070	.75	1.20	1.90	2.70	2.90	3.20	3.40	3.8	4.1	4.6	5.3	6.0	6.5	7.0	7.5	8.4	9.2	9.9
8	.072	.80	1.30	2.00	2.80	3.10	3.40	3.60	4.0	4.4	5.0	5.6	6.2	7.0	7.5	8.0	8.9	9.8	10.6
8.5	.074	.85	1.30	2.20	3.00	3.30	3.60	3.80	4.3	4.6	5.3	6.0	6.7	7.4	8.0	8.5	9.5	10.4	11.2
9	.076	.90	1.40	2.30	3.20	3.50	3.80	4.00	4.5	5.0	5.5	6.4	7.1	7.8	8.5	9.0	10.1	11.0	11.9
9.5	.078	.95	1.50	2.40	3.40	3.70	4.00	4.30	4.8	5.2	5.8	6.8	7.6	8.3	9.0	9.5	10.62	11.6	12.6
10	.080	1.00	1.60	2.50	3.50	3.90	4.20	4.50	5.0	5.4	6.1	7.0	8.0	8.7	9.4	10.0	11.2	12.2	13.2
12	.087	1.20	1.90	3.00	4.20	4.60	5.00	5.40	6.0	6.4	7.3	8.4	9.5	10.4	11.2	12.0	13.42	14.6	15.70
12.5	.089	1.25	1.98	3.13	4.42	4.84	5.23	5.59	6.25	6.85	7.65	8.84	9.88	10.83	11.69	12.50	13.98	15.3	16.5
13	.091	1.30	2.06	3.25	4.60	5.03	5.44	5.81	6.50	7.12	7.96	9.19	10.28	11.26	12.16	13.00	14.53	15.8	17.02
15	.094	1.50	2.40	3.80	5.30	5.80	6.40	6.80	7.5	8.2	9.2	10.6	12.0	12.9	14.0	15.00	16.8	18.4	19.8
20	.109	2.00	3.20	5.00	7.10	7.80	8.40	9.00	10.0	10.8	12.2	14.2	16.0	17.4	18.8	20.00	22.36	24.3	28
25	.125	2.50	3.95	6.25	8.84	9.68	10.46	11.18	12.50	13.69	15.31	17.68	19.76	21.65	23.39	25.00	27.95	30.4	35
30	.141	3.00	4.70	7.50	10.60	11.60	12.80	13.60	15.0	16.40	18.40	21.2	24.0	26.0	28.0	30.00	33.54	36.6	42
40	.156	4.00	6.30	10.00	14.20	15.60	16.80	18.00	20.0	21.60	24.40	28.4	32.0	34.8	37.6	40.00	44.72	48.75	56
50	.172	5.00	7.91	12.50	17.68	19.36	20.92	22.36	25.00	27.39	30.62	35.36	39.53	43.30	46.77	50.00	55.90	60.93	70
60	.188	6.00	9.49	15.00	21.21	23.24	25.10	26.83	30.00	32.86	36.74	42.43	47.43	51.96	56.12	60.00	67.08	73.11	84

Figure 3 Note: A commonly used standard for nozzle size is the "nozzle number" which is equivalent to the nozzle capacity in GPM at 4000 PSI. Spray angle does not affect nozzle volume.

As you can see, things are going to get interesting. But first we put aside the chart that I gave for an example. We must first know what our sprayer is going to be putting out in Gallons Per Minute (GPM) there are two ways to do this, but I have found over the years is the ounce method with the sprayer set at a specific RPM and the tank open and spraying as to be able to measure the output of at minimum 3 to 4 nozzles at least one per boom (normally the furthest from the input line).

GROUND SPEED CALCULATIONS AND DOES AND DON'TS

Generally, almost all of us use the first gear and throttle all the way up, giving us a typical ground speed of 3.5 MPH. If you are lucky enough to have a smart phone as

I do, your GPS will provide you with the exact or near exact speed you will be traveling. **A quick note to most newbies: FASTER IS NOT BETTER.** Traveling faster will allow for more drift, missing your target, less chemical being applied, and a waste of precious money by wasting chemical. I stress to my applicators that they maintain the proper set speed all the time to prevent these possible problems, the most important is drift. Off target drift may leave you liable to prosecution or fines and loss of license. It is also a danger to the environment. It also means that at faster speeds you generally apply less chemical, twice the speed equals half the rate.

Calibrating a boom sprayer is not as difficult as it sounds. Although there are many methods to use, the method described here is simple and requires few calculations. It's based on spraying 1/128 of an acre per nozzle and collecting the spray that would be released during the time it takes to spray the area. Because there are 128 ounces of liquid in 1 gallon, this convenient relationship results in ounces of liquid caught from one nozzle being directly equal to the application rate in gallons per acre, or GPA.

For example: If you catch an average of 15 ounces from a set of nozzles, the actual application rate of the sprayer is equal to 15 GPA. With this method, make sure that the time used to catch output from nozzles is the same as the time it takes to cover 1/128 acre. Table 1 shows the distance you must travel to cover 1/128 acre for different nozzle spacings and row spacings. For broadcast applications, use the nozzle spacing to determine the calibration distance.

Table 1. Calibration distance for each nozzle to spray 1/128 acre.			
Nozzle/row spacing (in.)	Travel distance (ft.)	Nozzle/row spacing (in.)	Travel distance (ft.)
18	227	30	136
20	204	32	127
22	185	34	120
24	170	36	113
26	157	38	107
28	146	40	102

To calibrate your sprayer, you need a measuring tape, a watch capable of indicating seconds, and a measuring jar graduated in ounces. A pocket calculator also will be handy.

Calibrating for Broadcast Application

Follow these steps when calibrating boom sprayers for broadcast applications:

1. **Fill the sprayer tank with water.** We do this because your sprayer will normally be full or will have chemical in it. You won't run an empty sprayer and the speeds will differ. The full sprayer accounts for wheel slippage, etc.

2. Run the sprayer, inspect it for leaks, and make sure all vital parts function properly.

3. Measure the distance in inches between the nozzles. Then measure an appropriate distance in the field based on this nozzle spacing, as shown in Table 1. Also travel in similar ground compared to what you are spraying, i.e. rolling terrain, bumpy roughs, etc.

4. Drive through the measured distance in the field at your normal spraying speed and record the travel time in seconds. Repeat this procedure and average the two measurements.

5. With the sprayer parked, run the sprayer at the same pressure level and catch the output from each nozzle in a measuring jar for the travel time required in Step 4.

6. Calculate the average nozzle output by adding the individual outputs and then dividing by the number of nozzles tested. If an individual sample collected is more than 10 percent higher or lower than the average nozzle output rate, check for clogs and clean the tip, or replace the nozzle.

7. Repeat steps 5 and 6 until the variation in discharge rate for all nozzles is within 10 percent of the average.

8. Then, the final average output in ounces is equal to the application rate in gallons per acre: Average output (ounces) = Application rate (GPA).

9. Compare the actual application rate with the recommended or intended rate. If the actual rate is more than 5 percent higher or lower than the recommended or intended rate, you must make adjustments.

10. You can start the adjustments by changing the pressure. Lowering the spray pressure will reduce the spray delivered; higher pressure means more spray is delivered. Don't vary from the pressure range recommended for the nozzles that you use.

11. You also can correct the application error by changing the actual travel speed. Slower speeds mean more spray is delivered; faster speeds mean less spray is delivered.

12. If these changes don't bring the application rate to the desired rate, then you may have to select a new set of nozzles with smaller or larger orifices.

13. Recalibrate the sprayer (repeat steps 5 through 12) after any adjustment.

Chart one gives you a simplified way to determine your travel speed. You may use this chart as it is time tested and used often. If a sprayer travels 1 mph faster or slower than required, it will under or over apply pesticides by 5-8 gallons per acre (based on 20 gallons per acre delivery rate, 3.5 MPH travel speed, 24" nozzle spacing). If an operator intends to apply 20 gallons per acre, this could result in an under or over application of 25-40%. This is quite a cost over time, especially with the rising cost of chemicals and fertilizers

Chart 1
Determine MPH By Seconds Required To Travel 200 Feet

Seconds per 200 Feet	68.2	54.5	45.5	39.0	34.1	30.3	27.3	24.8	22.7	21.0	19.5
Miles per Hour	2.0	2.5	3.0	3.5	4.0	4.5	5.0	5.5	6.0	6.5	7.0

To calculate speed:

MPH = 136.36 ÷ Seconds Required to Travel 200 Feet

DELIVERY RATE CALCULATIONS IN GALLONS PER MINUTE (GPM)

The number of gallons delivered per minute by a spray nozzle can be determined by collecting the output in ounces during 1 minute. A plastic container with a 60-ounce graduated capacity should be used. Do not add pesticide to the spray tank. Calibrate using only water and begin with the pressure gauge set at the appropriate pressure for the nozzles. Adjust the pressure to achieve the appropriate delivery rate. The following chart can be used to convert ounces-per-minute to gallons-per-minute. This procedure should be repeated for each nozzle on the boom.

Chart 2

Convert Ounces Per Minute to Gallons Per Minute

Ounces per Minute	14	16	18	20	22	24	26	28	30	32
Gallons per Minute	0.11	0.13	0.14	0.16	0.17	0.19	0.20	0.22	0.23	0.25

To calculate delivery rate:

GPM = Ounces Collected Per Minute ÷ 128

Each nozzle is designed to deliver a predetermined volume at a given pressure. For the nozzle to provide the appropriate application rate and develop the correct pattern, it must be supplied with an uninterrupted flow of tank liquid at the correct pressure. Identically sized nozzles should provide the same delivery rate. Old or cheap pressure gauges are frequently inaccurate. Rely on the spray pattern and delivery rate rather than the numerical gauge value.

SPRAY PATTERNS

If all of the nozzles on a boom sprayer are the same size and type, then the spray pattern and delivery rate should also be the same. When operating at the correct pressure, if a clean nozzle is above or below the correct delivery rate by 10% or more, then it should be replaced. For example, if a worn tip is designed to deliver 0.20 GPM and it delivers at or below 0.18 GPM or at or above 0.22 GPM, then it should be replaced. Also, if brass or plastic nozzles are being used and two or more nozzles show excessive wear, all nozzles of the same age should be replaced.

Determining spray pattern overlap and measuring uniformity of distribution can be difficult. Visual appraisal of the spray patterns while stationary equipment is operating at the correct pressure will frequently reveal problems. A new nozzle can also be installed for comparison. If the patterns are not the same or spray overlap is incorrect, this may be easily observed. Another way to visually appraise the spray pattern requires access to a large concrete or asphalt area such as a parking lot, driveway, or private road.

On a warm, calm, sunny day, while applying only water, spray a hard, flat surface for a distance of 20-30 feet. Make sure the boom sprayer is operating at the appropriate pressure and traveling at the correct speed. The sun should be shining evenly on the surface sprayed, and the surface should be free of debris and dirt. As soon as the test strip is sprayed, stop the spray rig and turn off the sprayer. Closely observe the wet area that was just sprayed. If the spray was applied uniformly, it should evaporate uniformly. For broadcast or band spraying, the wet areas should evaporate uniformly from start to finish. The boom may need to be positioned closer to the surface in some situations.

For broadcast spraying, if the moisture appears as stripes while evaporating, then the nozzles could be worn, the flow might be blocked, or the nozzle overlap, or boom height might be incorrect. This test will make it obvious if one or more nozzles are not operating correctly. Adjusting and/or replacing components will allow the spray evaporation test to result in fairly uniform evaporation. This is a subjective evaluation, with much room for interpretation and error. To achieve best results, the "spray and observe" process should be repeated three to four times, and the pattern carefully evaluated each time.

If problems are apparent, the malfunctioning nozzles should be cleaned or replaced. If worn, blocked, and/or damaged nozzles are used on a spray unit, the resulting outcome will reflect the pattern sprayed. Under-treated and over-treated areas will be obvious, and misapplications of materials such as herbicides can be easily recognized.

One thing I have done on my sprayer is added a back-up or rear camera to monitor sprayer nozzles while applying chemicals. Along with having a crew member checking every now and then, this will allow you to quickly identify a problem before it is to late.

APPLICATION RATE GALLONS PER ACRE(GPA) AND GALLONS PER MINUTE (GPM)

When applying a pesticide, it is important that label directions are followed. An applicator's failure to follow label directions can result in criminal penalties and/or fines. Do not exceed the application rate specified on the pesticide label. Read and follow the label directions. **Remember, the label is the law unless specified differently by your local and state laws.**

Spray operators commonly select a convenient pesticide application rate. Rates such as 10 or 20 gallons of mixture per acre are frequently selected. Higher rates, such as 20 gallons per acre, offer better coverage of the target site, while lower rates, such as 10 gallons per acre, provide greater field coverage per tank-full. Applicators should keep detailed records of pesticide dilutions, application rates, sprayer travel speed, pressure settings, spray sites, and results. Records are generally required by law. In Maine it is required to keep a complete pesticide record but not a fertilizer record. I recommend both for reference.

Chart 3

Determining Application Rate In Gallons Per Acre (GPA) And Gallons Per Minute (GPM)

Travel Speed	Nozzle Spacing	Application Rate	
MPH	Inches	GPA	GPM
3.5	20	10	0.12
3.5	20	20	0.24
3.5	24	10	0.14
3.5	24	15	0.21
3.5	24	20	0.28
4	20	10	0.13
4	20	20	0.27
4	24	10	0.16
4	24	15	0.24
4	24	20	0.32
4.5	20	10	0.15
4.5	20	20	0.30
4.5	24	10	0.18

4.5	24	15	0.27
4.5	24	20	0.36
5	20	10	0.17
5	20	20	0.34
5	24	10	0.20
5	24	15	0.30
5	24	20	0.40

To calculate application rate:

GPA = GPM x 5940 ÷ MPH ÷ Nozzle Spacing in Inches

GPM = GPA x MPH x Nozzle Spacing in Inches ÷ 5940

GPM x 128 = Ounces per Minute

When adjusting spray calibration equipment for optimum performance, spray pressure is adjusted for small changes in delivery rate; travel speed is increased or decreased for larger adjustments; and tip replacement is the preferred method for major changes in delivery rates.

Chart 4 provides a cheat sheet for pesticide and fertilizer applications per tank

Chart 4

Pesticide And Water Mixtures

Spray Tank Capacity	Application Rate, Water, & Pesticide	Pesticide Label Application Rate		Pesticide Required per Full Tank		
Gal.	Gal./Acre	Gal./Acre	Lb./Acre	Gal./Tank	Oz./Tank	Lb./Tank
400	20	0.2		4		
400	15	0.2		5.33		
400	10	0.2		8		
400	10	0.1		4		
200	20	0.2		2		
200	15	0.1		1.33		
200	10		0.25			5
100	15	0.1		0.67	85.3	
100	10	0.1		1	128	
100	10		0.25			2.5
25	10	0.1		0.25	32	
25	10		0.5			1.25
10	10		0.5			0.5

To calculate pesticide and water mixtures:

Acres Sprayed per Full Tank = Tank Capacity in Gallons ÷ Application Rate in GPA

Gallons of Pesticide per Full Tank = Acres Sprayed per Full Tank x Application Rate in GPA

Care should be taken when filling a spray tank so that the water supply is protected from contamination and back siphoning. Individuals mixing pesticides should wear the appropriate personal protective equipment (PPE) as specified by the product label.

A formula I use to find the quantity for total quantity is say I want to apply Tebuconazole at a rate of .6 oz per 1000 sq. feet. I have 3.5 acres of greens: .6 x 43.5 = 26.1 oz or rounded 26 oz. per acre. Then simply multiply by total acres of 3.5 equals 91.35 total oz. I will need 1.5 tanks knowing my spray rate so 91.35 divided by 1.5 = is 61 oz. in first tank and 30 oz. in second tank. I usually round to nearest whole unless using a growth regulator where minute oz. per acre is required. This will work with any area, which we will work on figuring in the next chapter, area calculations.

When applying fungicides, carry extra screens and have nozzles ready because many fungicides, especially the thicker milkier ones will clog nozzles

I always carry spare gloves, a welder's rod and tip cleaner   for cleaning the tips (don't force the tip cleaner through, just use to lightly push the clog through if you don't have extra nozzles), spare screens and since I have three nozzles per nozzle body, I can quickly change nozzles without cleaning, but it always pays to have spares.

DIFFERENT TYPES OF SPRAYERS AND TECHNIQUES

Two general types of sprayers are available for greenhouse application of pesticides: hydraulic and low-volume. There are many variations of these that fit particular crops or growing methods.

In the hydraulic sprayer, a pump supplies energy that carries spray material to the target (plant foliage). Water is the carrier and the pump creates the pressure at 40-1000 psi. Spray material is usually applied to "wet" or "drip." Nozzles on the boom or handheld gun break the spray into small droplets and direct it to the foliage.

In a low-volume (LV) sprayer, spray material in a water or oil carrier is injected into a high-speed air stream developed by a fan, blower or compressor. In most LV sprayers, a small pump is used to inject a concentrate pesticide solution into the air stream. The speed of the air stream may be as high as 200 mph. To get sufficient coverage, the air within the foliage canopy must be replaced with air that contains the pesticide. As the droplet size is much smaller, good coverage can be achieved with less chemical.

SPRAYER DIFFERENCES

One way to distinguish between a hydraulic sprayer and low-volume sprayer is by droplet size. Hydraulic sprayers produce a spray with most droplets in the 200-400-micron diameter range (thickness of the human hair is about 100 microns). Low-volume sprayers develop a mist (50-100 microns) or fog (0.05-50 microns). Small droplets from a mist or fog applicator can result in more uniform coverage and greater likelihood of contact with the insect or disease. In contrast to the hydraulic sprayer, spray material is usually applied to "glisten" as it is difficult to see the individual droplets on the leaf.

One disadvantage to smaller droplets is that they evaporate quicker when the humidity is low and may not reach the target. Another is that the tiny droplets tend to bounce or skip on the leaf surface. This can be overcome somewhat by adding a spreader and sticker.

TYPES OF HYDRAULIC SPRAYERS

A hydraulic sprayer contains the following components: tank, pump with agitator, pressure gauge, regulating valve, relief valve, control valves, piping and nozzles, power source and support frame.

COMPRESSED AIR SPRAYER

The smallest sprayers are hand-carried, compressed air sprayers. They contain a 1- to 5-gallon tank with an air pump in the top and a wand with a nozzle for directing the spray. Their best use is for spot treatment of small areas. In operation, the tank has to be pumped up frequently to maintain pressure, and the tank must be shaken to agitate the chemical.

BACKPACK SPRAYER

The tank in this sprayer holds about four gallons of material. A hand-operated pump pressurizes the spray material as the operator walks along, and the wand with nozzle directs the spray to the target. Its use is limited to small areas that can be reached from a walkway.

SKID-MOUNTED SPRAYER

With a tank size up to 200 gallons, these sprayers will fit onto an ATV or electric cart. They can also be mounted on wheels and pulled by hand or with a compact tractor. A small electric or gas engine powers the pump. The unit may contain a hose reel and gun or a boom with nozzles.

IRRIGATION BOOM SPRAYER

With increasing production in plug and cell trays, the use of the boom sprayer has become an important tool for getting uniform watering. By installing three-way turrets with nozzles for irrigation, misting and pesticide application, one piece of equipment serves multi-purposes. An alternate method is to add a pesticide application boom to the same transport cart. An independent mixing tank, pump, filter and valves are needed.

CENTRAL PESTICIDE APPLICATION SYSTEM

In gutter-connected ranges, it is possible to install a piping system that will deliver pesticides to any part of the greenhouse. Pesticide preparation and filtration are done in a mixing area. A single pump and piping that will handle the pressure developed are required. A hose can be easily attached to one or more outlets in each bay to apply the pesticide. The disadvantage is that the entire system must be drained and cleaned before changing to a new chemical.

LOW-VOLUME SPRAYERS

BACKPACK MIST BLOWER

A small gas engine and integral fan creates an air stream with a velocity of 100-200 mph. Concentrate spray injected into the air stream by a special nozzle is carried to the foliage by the air. The spraying technique is more complicated than with a hydraulic sprayer. The nozzle should be directed into the plant canopy to get good penetration and coverage, but it should be kept at least six feet away from the plants to avoid blast damage. The operator should visualize that all the air within the canopy must be replaced by the air from the mist blower.

ELECTROSTATIC SPRAYER

Compressed air, given a negative electric charge as it travels through the nozzle, forms spray droplets and carries them to the plants. This helps to create more uniformly sized particles that disperse well because they repel each other. Charged particles are attracted to leaves, metal and some plastics; when they strike a surface, these particles create a momentary overcharge that repels other particles. These other particles land elsewhere on the leaf, so there is more uniform coverage.

The simplest electrostatic sprayer is backpack-carried and contains a tank and spray gun. It requires an independent air supply to charge the tank. Other units are cart-mounted with an integral compressor powered by a gas engine or electric motor. Electrostatic sprayers work best if the spray distance is less than 15 feet.

ROTARY DISK SPRAYER

The spinning disk is used to impact and break a stream of water into droplets that are 60-80 microns in diameter. A variety of sizes are available for greenhouse use.

THERMAL FOGGER

This machine requires a specially formulated carrier that is mixed with the pesticide to improve uniformity of droplet size and distribution of the spray material. The carrier also decreases molecular weight, allowing the particles to float in the air for up to six hours, a disadvantage if you have to get into the greenhouse to care for the plants.

In the operation of a thermal fogger, the pesticide is injected into an extremely hot, fast-moving air stream that vaporizes it into fog particles. Moving from one end of a greenhouse to the other, a thermal fogger can cover in as little as 15 minutes. Air circulation from an HAF system will give more uniform coverage and better foliage penetration.

Temperature and humidity also affect the spray droplets. Because of the noise associated with the jet engine, hearing protection is recommended.

MECHANICAL FOGGER

Also called a cold fogger, this device uses a high-pressure pump (1,000-3,000 psi) and atomizing nozzles to produce fog-size particles. Distribution of the spray material is through a hand-held gun or external fan unit. With the fan unit, the distance and amount of area that can be covered depends on the capacity of the fan. Multiple units or settings may be needed to cover large areas.

As with other foggers, penetration and coverage may not be as good as with a mist or hydraulic sprayer. Droplets in the 30-micron size drop out of the air fairly quickly but droplets in the 5-micron size may evaporate or float in the air currents for hours. Small particles don't have the mass or velocity to move into heavy foliate; however, in most studies, good insect control has been achieved.

Safety is important when using spray equipment employing a high-pressure pump. Keep hands and arms away from the nozzle because at high pressure, spray particles can penetrate the skin very easily. (John W. Bartok)

BACKPACK SPRAYER CALIBRATION

CALIBRATION FOR TREATING SMALL LAND AREAS

If you are applying pesticide to an area measured in square feet, calibrate the sprayer by staking out a 1,000-square-foot test plot (for example, 20 feet × 50 feet) on a surface similar to the treatment site.

Step 1. Fill the sprayer tank half full with water (no pesticide)

Step 2. Record the number of seconds it takes to spray the test plot evenly while walking at a comfortable, steady pace. (It is a good idea to spray the test plot two or three times and figure the average time.)

Step 3. Stand still and spray into a container for the average time found in Step 2.

- The number of ounces collected equals the amount of spray delivered to 1,000 square feet.
- With this number you can calculate the amount of pesticide and water needed to treat the target area.

Example:

Apply herbicide to a lawn 40 feet × 65 feet

Area to be treated: 40 ft. × 65 ft. = 2,600 sq. ft.

Label application rate: $\dfrac{2 \text{ oz.}}{1{,}000 \text{ sq. ft.}}$

Test-plot time to cover 1,000 sq. ft. = 80 seconds

Amount of water collected in 80 seconds: 57 oz.

Sprayer output: 57 oz. per 1,000 sq. ft.

1. To determine the total spray mixture needed, set up the following ratio and cross multiply:

$$\frac{57 \text{ oz.}}{1{,}000 \text{ sq. ft.}} = \frac{X \text{ oz.}}{2{,}600 \text{ sq. ft.}}$$

X = 148.2 oz. (round off to 148).

2. To determine the amount of herbicide needed, set up the following ratio and cross multiply:

$$\frac{2 \text{ oz.}}{1{,}000 \text{ sq. ft.}} = \frac{X \text{ oz.}}{2{,}600 \text{ sq. ft.}}$$

X = 5.2 oz. of herbicide

3.   To treat the target area, a little more than 5 oz. of herbicide should be added to 143 oz. of water (148 – 5). Because there are 128 ounces in 1 gallon, this will mean adding 5 ounces of herbicide to 1.1 gal. of water (143/128 = 1.1 gallons of water).

CALIBRATION FOR TREATING SMALL TREES, SHRUBS AND ORNAMENTALS

In this situation, you will find out how much water is needed to treat an average plant. If the label says, "spray to wet", spray as if you were painting the plant with spray paint. Try to avoid over-application and minimize dripping of the pesticide off the plant. Add water (no pesticide) to the tank and pressurize it. Then record the number of seconds it takes to spray a representative plant thoroughly. Now spray water into a container for that length of time. Use this number to calculate the amount of water and product needed.

Example:

Apply insecticide to 18 azaleas in a plant bed.

Labeled rate = 3 ounces of insecticide per gallon of water.

Number of plants to treat = 18

Seconds to spray one average plant = 12.

Amount of water collected in 12 seconds = 10 oz.

1.   To determine the total spray mixture needed, multiply the total number of plants to treat by the amount of water collected to treat one plant.

18 × 10 oz. = 180 oz.

Convert ounces to gallons: $\dfrac{180}{128}$ = 1.4 gallons

2.   To determine the amount of insecticide needed, multiply the labeled rate by the total spray mixture.

$$\frac{3 \text{ oz.}}{\text{gal}} \times 1.4 \text{ gal.} = 4.2 \text{ oz.}$$

3.   Add a little more than 4 oz. of insecticide to 176 oz. of water (180 – 4) to treat 18 azaleas.

CHEMICAL STORAGE BUILDINGS

A well-designed and well-maintained chemical storage facility protects people from exposure, reduces the chances of environmental contamination, prevents damage to chemicals from temperature extremes and excess moisture, safeguards chemicals, and reduces the likelihood of liability. Proper handling and storage of pesticides and petroleum-based products are important to reduce risk of serious injury or death of an operator or bystander. Fires or environmental contamination may result in large fines, cleanup costs, and civil lawsuits if these chemicals are not managed properly.

- Storage buildings should have appropriate warning signs and placards.
- Develop an emergency response plan and educate all golf course personnel regarding emergency procedures on a regular basis.
- Individuals conducting emergency chemical cleanups should be properly trained under requirements of federal Occupational Safety and Health Administration (OSHA).
- Locate pesticide storage away from other buildings, especially fertilizer storage facilities.
- Floors of chemical storage buildings should be impervious and sealed with chemical-resistant paint.
- Floors of chemical storage buildings should have a continuous sill to contain spills and should not have a drain. A sump is acceptable.

- Shelving should be fabricated from plastic or reinforced metal. Metal shelving should be painted to avoid corrosion. Wood shelving should never be used because of its ability to absorb spilled pesticides.
- Automatic exhaust fans and an emergency wash area should be provided
- Locate fan and light switches outside the entrance to the building to facilitate ventilation of building before entrance of staff.
- Store chemicals in original containers. Never store them in containers that might be mistaken as packaging for food or drink.
- Arrange containers so the labels are clearly visible. Securely fasten loose labels to ensure containers and associated labels are kept together.
- Damaged labels should be replaced immediately.
- Store flammable chemicals separate from those that are non-flammable.
- Store liquid materials below dry materials to prevent any leaks from contaminating dry products.
- Ensure that oil containers and small fuel containers (service containers) are properly labeled and stored within the facility.
- Ensure that all containers are sealed, secured, and properly labeled. Use only regulatory agency-approved, licensed contractors for disposal.

PPE'S

Exposure to pesticides can be mitigated by practicing good work habits and adopting modern pesticide mix/load equipment (e.g., closed loading) that reduce potential exposure. PPE, such as specific types of clothing, goggles, respirators, etc., protects workers from exposure through one or more pathways: skin, eyes, oral ingestion, or respiratory tract. **Pesticide labels list legal requirements for minimum PPE.** SDS also provide information on appropriate PPE to wear while handling the product as formulated. To avoid contamination, PPE should not be stored in a pesticide storage area.

Most BMP's require the correct PPE to be worn by workers and anyone handling the chemicals. Most state tests also require you to know and pass the specific sections on PPE. Over all, I, and most superintendents I know, will require their employees to be licensed as applicator and wear all protective equipment. This is not a place to skimp on your budget. The guidelines listed below will guide you in selecting the PPE needed for a safe work environment.

- Provide adequate PPE for all employees who work with pesticides (including equipment technicians who service pesticide application equipment).
- Ensure that PPE is sized appropriately for each person using it.
- Make certain that PPE is appropriate for the chemicals used as listed on the pesticide label.
- Ensure that PPE meets rigorous testing standards and is not just the least expensive.
- Store PPE where it is easily accessible but not in the pesticide storage area.
- Forbid employees who apply pesticides from wearing facility uniforms home.
- Provide laundering facilities or uniform service for employee uniforms.
- The federal Occupational Safety and Health Administration (OSHA) requires employers to fit test workers who must wear tight-fitting respirators.
- Meet requirements for OSHA 1910.134 Respiratory Protection Program.

Area math is fairly simple when you use it regularly. To properly calculate the amount of chemical, fertilizer, or seed /sod you will need, you first need to determine the area. There is nothing square or exact round or simple about the design the architects have given us, but it is simple to break down the areas into manageable calculations.

If you will notice from your course score card or if you are really lucky, the course blueprints, most of the fairways are trapezoid or rectangular in shape. It is best to measure these off and save the measurements in a log book for reference if you do not have one. Do not rely on past measurements or statements from others except your superintendent who has already measured these out.

TRAPOZIDES

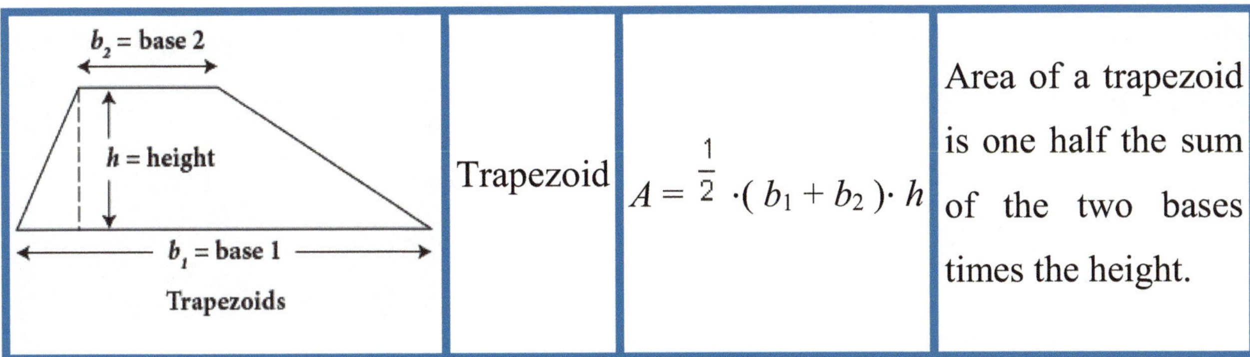

	Trapezoid	$A = \dfrac{1}{2} \cdot (b_1 + b_2) \cdot h$	Area of a trapezoid is one half the sum of the two bases times the height.

Finding the height (width) is fairly simply. Take your measuring wheel and walk the fairway from top to bottom and record. Walk with your wheel the length of the top of the fairway and record. Do the same for the bottom. For clarity, top is the right-hand side and bottom is the left-hand side. I go to the widest end to get my height (or width) which is usually near the tees but will be different on your course. I use the trapezoid measurement where possible because using a rectangular measurement will allow to much waste of chemical since there is to much rough area included in the measurement. The example below should simplify things a bit:

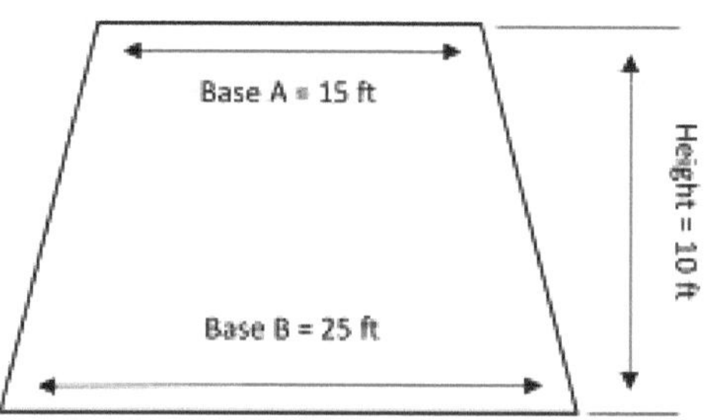

- Measure the length of each parallel side (Base A and B) in feet.
- Add the lengths together.
- Multiply the result by the height.
- Divide the result by 2

Example: 15' + 25'= 40 x 10'= 400 ÷ 2 = 200 sq. ft.

THE RECTANGLE AND SQUARE

This is one of the easiest to know and remember so a quick refresher in basic geometry is all we need here.

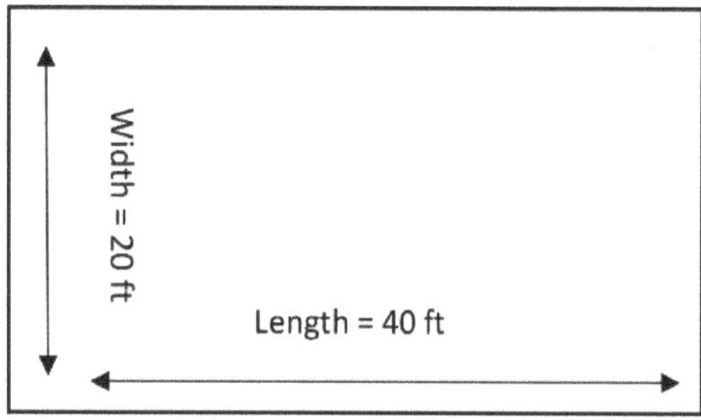

- Measure the length and the width of your area in feet.
- Multiply the two numbers together.

- Total is the square footage required.

Example: 20' x 40' = 800 sq. ft.

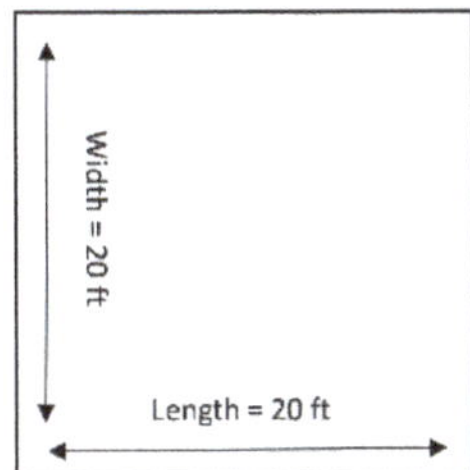

- your area in feet.
- Multiply the two numbers together.
- Total is the square footage required.

Example: 20' x 20' = 400 sq. ft.

See, pretty simple and easy to understand.

CIRCLES

A circle is a simple shape, consisting of those points in a plane that are a given distance from a given point - the center.

Origin: the center of a circle

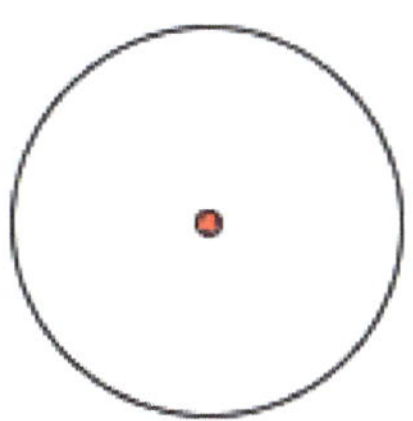

Radius: the distance from the center of a circle to any point on it.

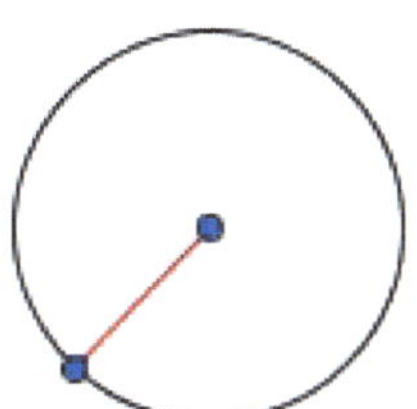

Diameter: the longest distance from one end of a circle to the other. The diameter = 2 × radius (d = 2r).

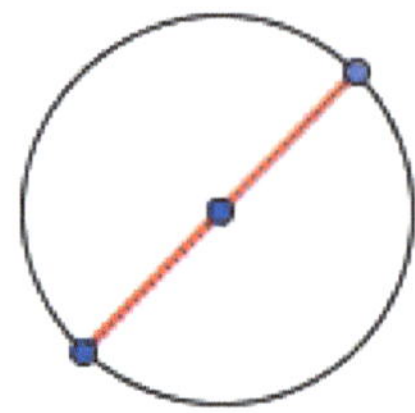

Circumference: the distance around the circle.

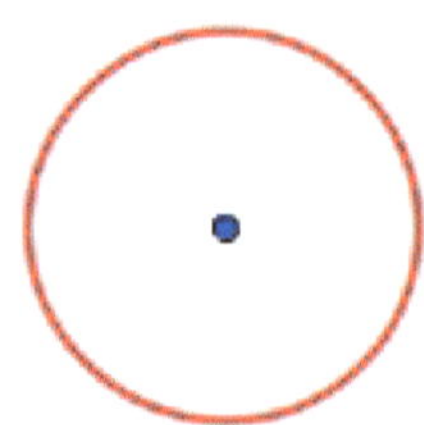

Circumference =π×diameter=π×diameter.

Circumference =π×d=2×π×r=π×d=2×π×r

π is equal to 3.14

Formulas

The formula for finding the **circumference** of a circle

is π·diameter=2·π·radiusπ·diameter=2·π·radius

The formula for finding the **area** of a circle is π·radius2π·radius2

The standard notation for a radius is *r*, for a diameter - *d*, for a circumference - **P** and for area **A**.

P=π·d=2·π·rP=π·d=2·π·r

A=π·r2

Practice these and you will find it is actually easier that it looks. Most calculators and constructions calculators have the basics built in and you just need to enter the numbers

MEASURING GREENS AND PONDS IRREGULAR SHAPES

How many of you have perfect circles for golf greens or ponds? Not many I assume. Typically, the best way to measure these is to divide them into shapes that are easier to measure, triangles, circles, rectangles. I will demonstrate below the best way that I know how to simplify this process, though this will take a bit of practice.

The method used for irregular shaped areas is called the "offset method". First measure the length of the longest axis of the area (line AB). This is called the *length line*. Next, divide the length line into equal sections, for example 10 ft. At each of these points, measure the distance across the area in a line perpendicular to the length line at each point (lines C through G). These lines are called *offset lines*. Finally, add the lengths of all offset lines and multiply the result times the distance that separates these lines (10 ft. in this example).

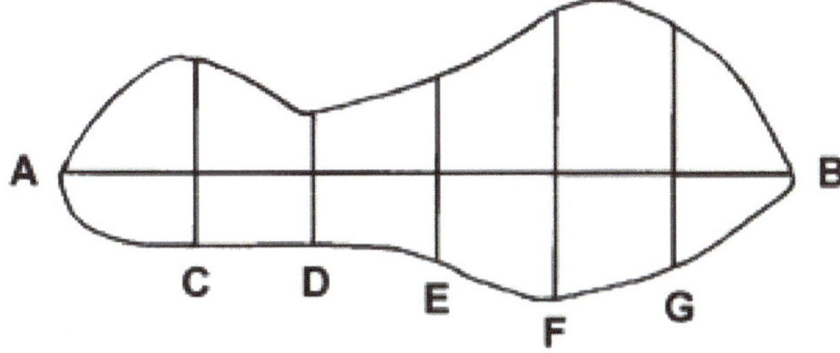

Example
Length line (AB) = 60 ft., distance between offset lines is 10 ft apart
• Length of each offset line
C = 15 ft, D = 10 ft, E = 15 ft, F = 25 ft, G = 20 ft

Total length of offset lines = C + D + E + F + G

- = 15 + 10 + 15 + 25 + 20

- = 85 ft

Area to fertilize = Distance between offset lines x sum of the length of the offset lines

- = 10 ft x 85 ft

- = 850 ft^2

The measurements used above represent both pond and greens measurements. Input your own numbers to find the right area calculation for your application. I use our club's yardage book because they have a good green drawing along with fairways which allows me to directly input the numbers and have a permanent record (provided you don't lose the book). If you don't have a yardage book, make one of your own using the scorecard as a basic template. You don't need to be an artist but getting a close shape will help you.

POND VOLUME

Along with finding areas of irregular shapes, I want to include finding pond volumes because there are times if you have an aquatics license that you will need to know the volume. You will also want to know this to calculate draw down of your irrigation ponds.

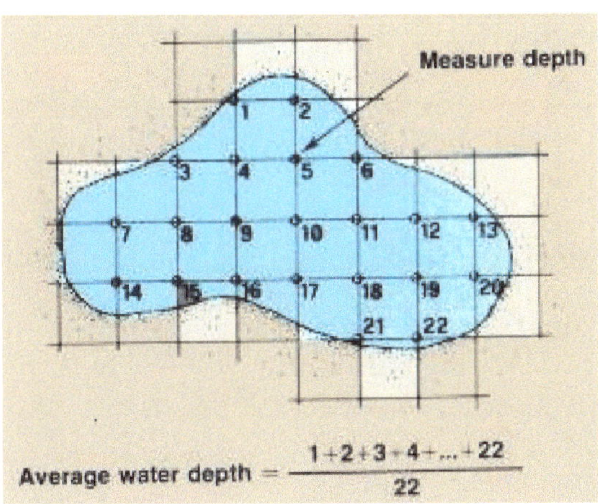

You have thus calculated the surface area of the pond and the average water depth of the pond. Now, using the figures you have found, you can calculate the volume of water in the pond by multiplying the surface in square feet (f^2) by the average water depth in feet (f) to get the volume of the pond in cubic feet (f^3).

SURFACE AREA x AVERAGE DEPTH = VOLUME

Cubic feet to gallons (ft3 to gal) volume units conversion factors are listed below. To find out how many gallons in cubic feet, multiply the cubic foot value by the conversion factor.

1 Cubic Foot = 7.48051948 Gallons [Fluid, US]

And there it is, finding total gallons in your irrigation pond. It is best to do this when full to determine loss due to evaporation and irrigation draw down.

You will need to know your local evaporation rate in order to calculate the amount of water lost from the surface of a pond by evaporation. Evaporation rates, which are provided by meteorological stations, are found by measuring and recording water losses by evaporation over many years.

One of the most common methods to find the evaporation rate is accurately to measure daily water losses from a standard-size container called a Class A Pan.

Evaporation rates by Class A Pan can be obtained from many meteorological stations throughout the world.

In choosing a meteorological station for evaporation rates, be careful to select one where climatic conditions such as sun, wind and rainfall are similar to conditions in your locality. If you are not sure ask the advice of a technician from the meteorological station.

Now all the fun stuff is over and it's time to move on to the stuff that all superintendents hate simply because it takes up vast amounts of time and we can't spray much anymore (unless we can push it off on a good assistant).

There are two budgets to concern ourselves with, the operating budget and the capital budget.

The operating budget addresses the ongoing, routine maintenance of the golf course, and includes expenses for labor, fertilizers, pesticides, equipment repair, fuel, supplies, utilities, leases (unless regarded as a purchase), and the like. Revenues from golf course fees generally fund the expenses in the golf course operating budget. The operating budget will project the current year's expenses and may be broken down on a month by month basis. The manger and owner can use the operating budget to compare the current year's expenses with the budget to project anticipated savings or losses. This budget may also be used to compare the current year's projections to previous years' expenses.

The capital budget addresses the acquisition of assets, and includes the construction of the golf course, construction of buildings and permanent fixtures, the purchases of equipment, and the like. Revenues from the sale of property and initiation fees, as well as windfall profits generally fund the capital budget. This budget should look forward at least two or three years, if possible, in order to plan for the financing necessary to keep the property and equipment in good repair. Failure to plan for these large ticket items on an annual basis may lead to an excessive, one-time expense to replace equipment or buildings and may result in diminished conditions and quality on the golf course.

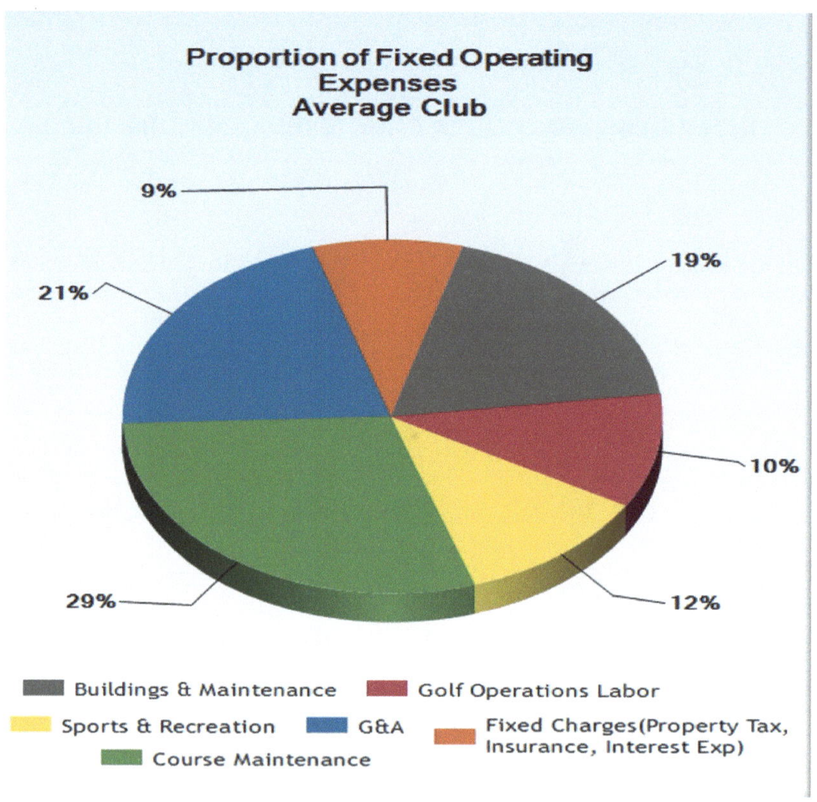

Figure 5 Percentage pie chart from my courses operating budget

THE ZERO – BASED BUDGET

The budget process starts with all line items being zero. Labor, based on predicted activities can constitute the beginning of the process. The standards and cycle-times should yield an hourly total for routine maintenance. Labor dollar amounts should be relatively simple to assign to job tasks; for instance, mowing greens would not require a high wage earner to accomplish, while applying fertilizers and chemicals to green surfaces will require a more experienced, higher wage earner.

Advantages of Goal Directed Budgeting:

1. Efficient allocation of resources, as it is based on needs and standards

2. Drives managers to find cost effective ways to improve standards and operations

3. Detects inflated budgets

4. Useful for golf course maintenance operations where the output is difficult to recognize

5. Increases motivation by providing greater initiative and responsibility in decision-making

6. Increases communication and coordination within the club's organization

7. Identifies and eliminates wasteful and obsolete operations

8. Identifies opportunities for outsourcing

9. Forces cost centers to identify their mission and their relationship to overall goals

Disadvantages of Goal Directed Budgeting:

1. Must define standards and decision units, which is time-consuming

2. Forced to justify every detail related to expenditures

3. Necessary to train managers. Goal Directed budgeting must be clearly understood by managers at
various levels to be successfully implemented.

4. The volume of information may be so large that compressing the information down to a usable size
might remove important details to middle and lower management

5. Honesty of the managers must be reliable and uniform - any manager that exaggerates input information skews the results

Labor costs probably will be the largest line item in the operating budget, and will include salaries~ wages, taxes, and benefits. In order to effectively plan and project labor costs, the owner and manager must agree upon the number of employees needed to maintain the golf course, how many employees will be full and part time, the wage and salary scale, what benefits will be offered, etc.

A simple spreadsheet will help plan and project wages and salaries. Once you know the number of employees you need, determine the number of weeks and the number of hours per week they will be working, including overtime hours. These numbers will obviously change from employee to employee as you consider your full-time people and any part time and summer staff that you may have.

You will then need to calculate the employer's liability for FICA, Medicare, and Unemployment Insurance, based on your projected gross salaries. Finally, do not forget to calculate Worker's Compensation Insurance, and any owner sponsored benefit plans offered to your employees when you are projecting total labor costs.

Mio Country Meadows
Golf Course Maintenance Budget

Account Description	January	February	March	April	May	June	July	August	September	October	November	December	Account Total	Percentage	
Salaries & Wages	$5,675	$5,700	$7,300	$8,500	$10,900	$11,900	$11,900	$11,900	$8,500	$7,300	$7,300	$5,675	$102,550	56.1%	
Payroll Taxes	1,419	1,425	1,825	2,125	2,725	2,975	2,975	2,975	2,125	1,825	1,825	1,419	$25,638	14.0%	
Health Insurance & Benefits	500	500	500	500	500	500	500	500	500	500	500	500	$6,000	3.3%	
Uniforms	200	200	200	200	200	200	200	200	200	200	200	200	$2,400	1.3%	
Gasoline & Lubricants	0	0	300	300	300	500	500	500	500	500	300	0	$3,700	2.0%	
Electricity	100	100	100	100	300	600	900	900	300	100	100	100	$3,700	2.0%	
Heating Fuel Costs	250	250	250	100	100	0	0	0	100	150	200	250	$1,650	0.9%	
Seed & Sod Supplies	0	0	0	0	100	250	300	300	250	0	0	0	$1,200	0.7%	
Fertilizers	0	0	0	1200	1200	2000	2000	2000	1200	1200	0	0	$10,800	5.9%	
Insecticides	0	0	0	0	0	0	300	300	0	0	0	0	$600	0.3%	
Herbicides	0	0	0	0	500	500	0	0	0	0	0	0	$1,000	0.5%	
Fungicides	0	0	0	0	0	500	500	600	600	2500	0	0	$4,700	2.6%	
Top Soil	0	0	0	0	500	500	500	0	0	0	0	0	$1,500	0.8%	
Sand & Gravel	0	0	0	0	0	500	600	500	0	0	0	0	$1,600	0.9%	
Expendable Supplies	100	100	100	100	100	100	100	100	100	100	100	100	$1,200	0.7%	
Irrigation R & M	0	0	0	0	0	300	300	300	100	0	0	0	$1,000	0.5%	
Equipment R & M	1000	1000	1000	1000	500	500	500	500	500	500	1000	1000	$9,000	4.9%	
Building R & M	100	100	100	100	100	100	100	100	100	100	100	100	$1,200	0.7%	
Miscellaneous	120	120	120	120	120	120	120	120	120	120	120	120	$1,440	0.8%	
Education Expenses	1200	300	50	50	50	50	50	50	50	50	50	50	$2,000	1.1%	$182,878
Monthly Totals:	$10,664	$9,795	$11,845	$14,395	$18,195	$22,095	$22,345	$21,845	$15,245	$15,145	$11,795	$9,514	$182,878	100.0%	
	5.8%	5.4%	6.5%	7.9%	9.9%	12.1%	12.2%	11.9%	8.3%	8.3%	6.4%	5.2%	100.0%		
	4,989	4,095	4,545	5,895	7,295	10,195	10,445	9,945	6,745	7,845	4,495	3,839	80,328		
													$128,188		
													$54,690		

Figure 6 Copy of the GCSAA budget template

In the picture above, you will notice that the payroll taxes and salary and wages make up about 60% of the actual budget. This budget is hypothetical and can be found on the GCSAA web site along with other helpful hints and articles concerning budgeting. Our main concern here is how we got to the numbers we will be working with.

The best way to identify future payroll costs is with past or historical analysis. Use past years' payroll records with a breakdown of each payroll cost as a reference of how much costs are involved and set a budget ceiling. The amount to pay your employees can take up a considerable portion of your payroll costs. The most basic compensation would be salaries and regular hourly wages. Other types of compensation might include payment to ad-hoc workers or part-timers. On top of the basic wages, employers have to take into consideration additional costs such as overtime pay, commissions, bonuses, severance pay, paid annual leaves, business expenses reimbursements and many others. If you realize that there are certain payroll items that are continuously bursting that budget, minimize or eliminate it. For instance, if you are unable to offer a three months' bonus to all employees, keep it at a minimum. Identify which are the key benefits that employees want. That way, you are able to budget your payroll costs appropriately without exceeding it.

And don't forget taxes and insurance. Employees' taxes and insurance for workers' compensation are typically mandatory under state law. Ensure that all employees are properly classified before doing estimated calculations on the taxes that your organization is required to pay. These classifications are exempt and non-exempt. In other words, salaried and non-salaried. Be careful on this classification and read the IRS laws to make sure people are classified correctly. You don't want to run a risk of an employee audit.

Factor in additional tax payments such as employment training tax. As a rule of thumb, ensure that all tax records, employment training records or insurance contracts are properly recorded and filed. This will allow you to set aside sufficient funds from your payroll budget to cover these costs.

Changes in the economy has a direct impact on employees' wages and payroll costs. As such, it is critical that you take into consideration the cost of living for the particular year into the estimated payroll budget. Additionally, the flow of new hires and resignations can play a significant role in your payroll budget. Estimate the organization's attrition rate and factor the percentage in when calculating salary increase. Taking these aspects into consideration will allow you to increase employees' salaries without a substantial increase in your payroll budget.

Remember that there is no magical percentage that you should follow when setting your payroll budget. Keep in mind that there is no one size fits all and the budgeting process varies from company to company. Instead, determine which are the real costs of your employees and where unnecessary costs can be reduced to prevent exceeding of your payroll budget.

First	Last	Rate	Hours (est monthly)	1/1/2013	2/1/2013	3/1/2013	4/1/2013	5/1/2013	6/1/2013	7/1/2013	8/1/2013	9/1/2013	10/1/2013	11/1/2013	12/1/2013
Seth	David			500.00	500.00	500.00	750.00	750.00	750.00	750.00	-	-	-	-	-
Doug	Sleeter			1,000.00	1,000.00	1,000.00	1,000.00	1,000.00	1,000.00	1,000.00	1,000.00	1,000.00	1,000.00	1,000.00	1,000.00
Sherrill	Sleeter			1,500.00	1,500.00	1,500.00	1,500.00	1,500.00	1,500.00	1,500.00	1,500.00	1,500.00	1,500.00	1,500.00	1,500.00
Tom	Sleeter			750.00	750.00	750.00	750.00	750.00	750.00	750.00	750.00	750.00	750.00	750.00	750.00
Nathan	Fochler			250.00	250.00	250.00	250.00	250.00	250.00	250.00	250.00	250.00	250.00	250.00	250.00
Jeannie	Reusch			100.00	100.00	100.00	100.00	100.00	100.00	100.00	100.00	100.00	100.00	100.00	100.00
New1				-	-	500.00	500.00	500.00	500.00	500.00	500.00	500.00	500.00	500.00	500.00
New2				-	-	-	-	-	400.00	400.00	400.00	400.00	400.00	400.00	400.00
New3				-	-	-	-	-	-	-	-	-	-	-	-
New4				-	-	-	-	-	-	-	-	-	-	-	-
New5				-	-	-	-	-	-	-	-	-	-	-	-
Total Monthly Compensation				4,100.00	4,100.00	4,600.00	4,850.00	4,850.00	5,250.00	5,250.00	4,500.00	4,500.00	4,500.00	4,500.00	4,500.00
Emplyee Count				6.00	6.00	7.00	7.00	7.00	8.00	8.00	7.00	7.00	7.00	7.00	7.00
Other Expenses Related to Payroll															
SS/Mcare	7.65%			313.65	313.65	351.90	371.03	371.03	401.63	401.63	344.25	344.25	344.25	344.25	344.25
Workers Comp	1.50%			61.50	61.50	69.00	72.75	72.75	78.75	78.75	67.50	67.50	67.50	67.50	67.50
Health Insurance	3	275.00		-	-	-	1,650.00	1,650.00	1,925.00	1,925.00	1,925.00	2,200.00	2,200.00	1,925.00	1,925.00

Figure 7 Example of a typical monthly budget

MS Excel is an amazing and powerful small business productivity tool. I know there are all kinds of budget apps and dashboard tools out there but when it comes down to it, none of them measure up to Excel when you really know how to play around in Excel to get the things that you need done.

With a simple layout and a couple of well written formulas you can have your financial cake and eat it too, and **you don't have to go out and buy an expensive app**. You just have to have the patience (mainly with yourself) to learn something new.

- The first part is easy. Open a new Excel Workbook and get to a clean sheet.

- Then start listing your existing employees (name only). You can break it up by First and last in 2 separate columns if you like. This can be helpful later if you want to sort by Last name.
- The next part is where you want to lay out the months as a header on a line above where the first name appears. Leave a few columns in between. You'll see why later.
- Fill in each employee's monthly compensation. The extra columns are there in case you have hourly employees, so you can calculate it based on an average (assumption) # of hours per month * their rate.
- Leave space for new employees and then set up a total line.
- Then 2 rows below the total we want to set up a line item to give us an employee count.
- Next create a section for "Other Expenses" and set up line items for the following:
    - Social Security * Medicare
    - Workers Comp
    - Health Insurance
    - Any other expenses that are driven by payroll costs/employees.

This is how I typically run my employee spread sheet. I also have a spread sheet set for weekly pays since we pay on a weekly basis. I can then transfer from one 'book' to another in my spread sheet program. Get used to this system and report writing and cost analysis will be a breeze.

Plan for purchasing new equipment and equipment maintenance in the annual budget planning. Budgeting for purchasing and maintenance of equipment must be done to be better able to finance this when this is needed.

Equipment depreciation:
- Write down for each piece of equipment:
  - The estimated costs per year for maintenance of the piece of equipment.
  - The estimated date on which the piece of equipment will have to be replaced because it is getting too old.
  - The estimated price of a new piece of equipment replacing the old one.
- Divide the price of a new piece of equipment that will replace the old one over the number of years remaining between now and the expected replacement date. This is the equipment depreciation cost for this piece of equipment.
- Calculate the amount of money that should be set aside each year for the piece of equipment by adding the yearly equipment depreciation cost to the yearly costs for equipment maintenance.
- Do this for each piece of equipment present.
- Calculate the sum of yearly equipment depreciation costs for all equipment present. Include these costs in the budget for the next year under the expense "Equipment depreciation".
- Calculate the sum of yearly maintenance costs for all equipment present. Include these costs in the budget for the next year under the expense "Equipment preventive maintenance".
- Make an estimation of the yearly costs of equipment repair; as repair is often unexpected it is not possible to know the exact amount of money needed for

the next year. However, try to make a rough estimation of the average amount of money spent on equipment repair over the last years and include this amount in the budget for next year under the expense "Expected equipment repair".

Try to anticipate break down of old equipment by identifying which pieces of equipment will not last long anymore and start to look for funding to have replacements ready before these pieces of equipment break down.

New equipment:

- When making the yearly budget, see if you will need to buy new equipment next year.
- Include the estimated price for this equipment in the budget, considering shipping and installation costs (under the expense "New equipment purchases").

Include also an expense for unexpected equipment repairs when equipment breaks down. Determine what is a reasonable amount of money so that for the average equipment repair there is always enough money available.

The best way I have found is to break down each piece of equipment and log it into an excel spread sheet. I label each piece of equipment, hours at start of year and end of year, any major repairs and cost of break down. Your mechanic should also keep a log book on each piece to help determine when a piece of equipment is reaching its end of life or when repairing is becoming to costly to keep that piece of equipment running.

Determining when to buy a piece of equipment has many factors determining it. The main ones are if allocated in budget which you will have done by following the above information. The next is how much down time and mechanic wages are going into one piece of equipment as compared to a newer piece. You will also look at the costs of parts replacement. As the equipment gets older, parts prices get higher when it is hard to find. Add all this together and you may find it is less expensive to invest in equipment to reduce costs.

SEED CALCULATIONS

Select the grass seed you will use to establish or overseed the turf area. The seeding rate varies depending on the cultivar or blend and is usually specified by the seed provider or on the bag of seed. For example, if you wish to plant a new Kentucky bluegrass lawn, the seeding rate is 2 to 3 pounds of seed per 1,000 square feet. If you are planting a tall fescue lawn, the recommended rate is 8 to 10 pounds per 1,000 square feet.

Convert the seeding rate for the chosen grass cultivar or blend from pounds per 1,000 square feet to pounds per acre, if needed. For example, if the recommended seeding rate for a specific blend of grasses is 6 pounds per 1,000 square feet, multiply 6 by 43.56 to get 261.36. Thus, you would need just over 261 pounds of seed for 1 acre.

Measure or estimate the dimensions of any non-turf areas in the landscape, calculate their areas and add the square footage of all of the non-turf areas together.

Convert the square footage of any non-turf areas to acreage and subtract the non-turf areas from the acreage of the entire site. For example, if you have a 1-acre yard where the house, driveway, flower beds and other landscaping create a combined area of 20,000 feet, divide this amount by 43,560 (the number of square feet in an acre) and subtract this amount from 1 to determine that the acreage of the planned turf is about .54.

Calculate the amount of seed needed by multiplying the seeding rate in pounds per acre by the estimated acreages. For example, if the size of the planned turf area is .54 acre, multiply this by the determined seeding rate per acre, for example 261.36, to calculate a total of 142 pounds of seed.

Tips

- Always round up when making your calculations or purchase slightly more seed than you plan to use to avoid needing to purchase more (usually 5 to 10%), if you accidentally spill seed or spread it unevenly or have to overseed small areas.
- If the chosen grass seed has a low seeding rate, consider blending it with sand or sawdust to ensure more uniform spreading.

Warning

- Some grass seed or seed mixture is blended and packaged with other, non-grass seed material. Make sure you read the label on the bag of grass seed carefully and use the seed weight as listed on the label, not the total weight of the mixture, as a guide when purchasing seed.

Below is a standard seeding rate chart for most common turf grasses with greens and tees using bent grass listed below:

Standard Seeding Rates		
Kentucky Bluegrass - pasture	14	20-30
Tall Fescue	24	15-20
Annual Ryegrass	24	25-30

Perennial Ryegrass	24	25-30
Lawn Mixtures		125-300 3-8 lbs. / 1,000 sq. ft.
Kentucky Bluegrass - lawn	14	100-175
Fine Leaved Perennial Rye - lawn	24	5-8 lbs. / 1,000 sq. ft. 200-325
Creeping Red Fescue - lawn	14	125-200
Turf Type Fescue - lawn	24	200-325 5-8 lbs. / 1,000 sq. ft.

Seed for golf courses

Greens

Creeping bentgrass 100% at 1 lb. per 1,000 sq. ft

Tees and Fairways

Creeping bentgrass 100% at 1 lb. per 1,000 sq. ft

Perennial ryegrass 100% at 4–5 lb. per 1,000 sq. ft

SOD CALCULATIONS

To calculate how much sod you need to cover your lawn, you need to determine the square footage by multiplying width x length. If you have multiple rectangular surfaces, simply add them up.

Sod is sold in 1 Yard rolls, and to determine the number of rolls needed, take the square footage of the area you calculated by multiplying width x length and divide it by 9 to get 1 Yard rolls (standard). Consider adding 5-10% for cutting and trimming depending on the shape of your lawn.

Properly working systems are necessary for efficient irrigation. Irrigation audits can be conducted to assess the system function, ensuring that the irrigation system works reliably and cost effectively. The following are common measures of system performance used in irrigation audits:

Coefficient of Uniformity (CU). CU measures system performance by how widely a system varies in distribution. A CU of 100% means that a system is uniform. A CU of 84% or better is considered acceptable for high value products. Because the CU is calculated with the absolute value of the deviations, the score does not indicate whether the system is over- or under-watering. In addition, the score does not indicate what section of the area tested is not performing.

Distribution Uniformity of the Lowest Quartile (DULQ). The most commonly used calculation to determine uniformity of a sprinkler layout, DULQ is the ratio of the average measurements in the lowest 25% of samples to the overall average of all samples expressed as a percentage. For example, a DULQ of 60% means that the lowest 25% of the samples measured only received 60% of the average water applied. Some resources suggest that a DULQ of 65% or less is poor, 75% is good, and 85% or more is excellent.

Scheduling Coefficient (SC): measures the average water applied to the driest, most critical areas of an area under test and compares to the average. An SC of 100% implies the distribution is uniform. An SC of 120 % indicates that the average was 120% more water applied than the driest area. The SC is often used to adjust run times to ensure that the driest areas receive the required scheduled water replacement. The disadvantage of this method is that all other areas receive 20% too much water, increasing the risk of runoff and leaching.

An irrigation audit can be conducted for any location on the golf course (greens, tees, fairways) that receives overhead irrigation. The audit process involves recording various site characteristics and then conducting a test to determine how uniform the irrigation system is applying water to the area being tested. Information such as the sprinkler type, arc adjustment, nozzle size, operating pressure, head spacing, and soil type are examples of site characteristics that are typically recorded. The uniformity is determined by placing a series of catch cans in a grid pattern across the area to be tested and then running the irrigation system for a specified amount of time.

The pictures below are from an irrigation audit I recently conducted. In the first picture you can see the catch cans placed across the green in a grid pattern. The distance between the catch devices will depend on the size of the area you are testing. We used heavy duty cups as our catch device for this audit and they were placed on 15-foot centers. Any object can be used to collect the irrigation water as long as all the objects are the same and you can measure the size of the opening of each catch device.

The irrigation system is then run for a specified amount of time and water is collected in each catch device. The amount of time the system is operated depends on the type of irrigation heads. In this audit the heads were gear driven rotors and the system was run for 10 minutes. The amount of water collected in each catch can is recorded once the cycle is complete.

Below you can see the results from this audit. The values from each catch device are used to calculate the Distribution Uniformity of the area. The DU represents how uniformly water is applied to the area and is expressed as a decimal. A DU value of 1.0 would represent complete uniformity within the area tested. For rotary sprinklers, the Irrigation Association considers DU values of 0.8 Excellent (Achievable) and 0.7 Good (Expected). Values below 0.55 are considered Poor and action should be taken.

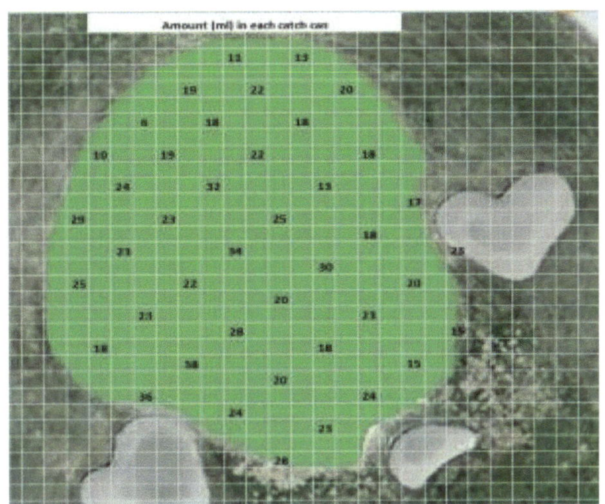

The calculated DU for this golf green was 0.63. The obvious question now becomes what can I do to improve the overall efficiency of the system? Performing regular maintenance activities such as leveling sprinkler heads, adjusting arcs for matched precipitation rates, checking and replacing clogged or worn nozzles and drive mechanisms are all practices that will help. The results of the audit may alter you to problems that require more significant repairs such as moving sprinkler heads to appropriate spacings, adjusting water pressure (up or down), or even upgrading various system components.

CALCULATING DU

Catch-can test. This simple test can tell you the uniformity of distribution and precipitation rate (how fast water is being applied). A catch can is any can that has straight sides and a flat bottom. A coffee can is ideal. On a calm morning, place 16 to 20 catch cans in the fairway. Test an area where you have head-to-head coverage. Place one-third of the cans near the heads, one-third towards the edge of the radius of throw and one-third in the middle. Sketch a map of catch-can placement to record the data on.

Run the irrigation system for 30 minutes. Ideally, you want to catch an inch of water in the cans. Measure the depth of water with a ruler or tape. If you have not collected an inch of water, continue irrigating for a total of 60 minutes. When complete, measure the depth of each catch can in millimeters and record on the map. After you've taken all the measurements, you can determine the distribution uniformity.

DU is a measurement of uniformity. Rank the catch-can measurements from highest to lowest. Take the average of the lowest 25 percent of readings. For example, if you had 20 measurements, the bottom 5 should be used. Divide the average of the lowest 25 percent by the average of all of the measurements (in this case, the average of all 20 measurements). Multiply this number by 100 to get the distribution uniformity percentage.

The higher the percentage, the more uniform the distribution of water applied. As a guideline, 70 percent or higher is satisfactory. If DU is below 70 percent, observe the map for areas of low application. Are nozzles worn excessively? Are the heads level? Is there adequate spacing and adequate pressure?

PRECIPITATION RATE (PR).

 Most superintendents have a good feel for how long to run each head. Using the PR, you can schedule heads to run according to the amount of water that needs to be replaced. You can obtain evapotranspiration (ET) rates (water loss) by installing a weather station on your site or subscribing to a service that calculates this information for your area.

PR is measured in inches of water delivered per hour. Convert the catch-can measurements to inches by dividing the measurements by 25.4. Then take an average of all the measurements. Next, convert the amount of water caught in the catch can to a per-hour reading. For instance, if the catch-can test was run for 30 minutes, double the average. If the test was run for an hour, this is the PR per hour of your system. For example, if the overall average of a 30-minute test was 0.44 inches, then the PR (inches per hour) of your system would be 0.88 inches.

To use the PR, divide the ET rate (amount of water lost) by the PR to determine how long you need to operate your irrigation system to replace the amount of water lost. If you water every other day, calculate how much water you have lost after 2 days. For this example, the water loss is 0.70 inch for 2 days.

Use these numbers and record them regularly. These will give you an indication is something is starting to go wrong or if you see something you will know if it is irrigation or another hidden problem. I use a monthly audit to keep track of my usage along with my computerized system to help me determine if there is a possible small breakage in the irrigation system. It is also a good idea to have these numbers when you go to the Greens Committee or owners for a new system.

Useful Conversions, Area Determination, and Topdressing Calculations for Landscapes

Length

1 inch (in) = 2.54 centimeters (cm) or 25.4 millimeters (mm)

1 cm = 0.3937 in

1 foot (ft) = 12 in = 304.8 mm = 30.48 cm = 0.3048 meters (m)

1 yard (yd) = 3 ft = 36 in = 0.914 m

Area

1 square foot (ft2

) = 144 square inches (in2

)

1 square yard (yd2

) = 9 ft2

1 square meter (m2

) = 10.76 ft2

1 acre (ac) = 43,560 ft2 = 4,480 yd2 = 4,046.9 m2 = 0.40469 hectares (ha)

1 hectare (ha) = 10,000 m2 = 2.471 ac

Weight

1 ounce (oz) = 28.35 grams (g)

1 pound (lb) = 16 oz = 453.6 g = 0.4536 kilograms (kg)

1 kg = 2.205 lbs

1 gallon (gal) of water = 8.3356 lbs

1 cubic ft (ft3

) of water = 62.36 lbs

Liquid

1 tablespoon (tbsp) = 3 teaspoons (tsp) = 15 milliliters (ml) = 0.5 fluid ounces (fl oz)

1 fl oz = 29.6 ml = 2 tbsp = 1.805 cubic inches (in3)

1 cup = 8 fl oz = 16 tbsp

1 pint (pt) = 2 cups = 16 fl oz = 473 ml

1 quart (qt) = 2 pt = 4 cups = 32 fl oz

1 gallon (gal) = 4 qt = 16 cups = 8 pt = 128 fl oz = 3.785 liters (l)

1000 ml = 1 liter

Volume

1 cubic centimeter (cc, cm3

) = 0.061023 in3

1 cubic in (in3

) = 16.387 cm3

1 cubic yard (yd3) = 27 ft3 = 46,656 in3 = 764,559.4 cm3

DETERMINING AREA

Square or Rectangle

Area = LW

L = Length

W = Width

Area = 50 ft × 105 ft = 5250 ft2

Circle or near Circular

Area = πr2

π = 3.14

r = radius

Area = 3.14 × 30 ft × 30 ft = 2,826 ft2

Ovals or Egg Shapes (within 5% accuracy)

Area = 0.8LW

L = Length

W = Width at Mid-Point

Area = 0.8 × 105 ft × 50 ft = 4,200 ft2

Triangle

Area 0.5BH

B = Base

H = Height

Area = 0.5 × 210 ft × 200 ft = 21,000 ft2

r = 30 ft

W = 50 ft

L = 105 ft

L = 105 ft

W = 50 ft

H = 200 ft

B = 210 ft

G VOLUME (for Topdressing)

Volume = LWD

L = Length

W = Width

D = Depth (or Height)

Example 1:

How many cubic yards (yd3) of yard-waste compost topdressing needed to provide a ¼-inch (0.25-inch) layer on a lawn that measures 200-ft long by 55-ft wide (11,00ft2 or 1,221 yd2)?

Need the same units for all measurements (convert all to yd)

0.25 inch = 0.00694 yd (obtained from 0.25 ÷ 36)

200 ft = 66.7 yd (obtained from 200 ÷ 3)

55 ft = 18.3 yd (obtained from 55 ÷ 3)

Volume = LWD = 66.7 yd × 18.3 yd × 0. 00694 yd = ≈8.5 yd3

Or could multiply the known area (in yd2) by the depth (in yd):

1,221 yd2 × 0.00694 yd = ≈8.5 yd3

If topdressing is sold by the ton (2,000 lbs.), and assuming the bulk density of yard-waste compost is about 800lbs. per yd3, then:

8.5 yd3 × 800 lbs. per yd3

= 6,800 lbs.

6,800 lbs. ÷ 2,000 lbs. per ton = ≈3.5 tons of yard-waste compost

(NOTE: compost bulk density can vary greatly depending on moisture content; get an estimate of the bulk density of the material you are using before you apply)

Example 2:

How much sand topdressing needed (yd3) to provide a ⅛-inch (0.125-inch) layer on a sports field that measures 125 yd long by 60 yd wide?

Need the same units for all measurements

0.125 inch = 0.0035 yd (obtained as 0.125 ÷ 36)

Volume = LWD = 125 yd × 60 yd × 0.0035 yd = 26.25 yd3

Or could multiply a known area by the depth needed:

7,500 yd2 × 0.0035 yd = 26.25 yd3

Usually sand topdressing is sold by the ton (2,000 lbs). If the bulk density of dry sand is about 100 lbs per ft3 then:

26.25 yd3 × 27 ft3 per yd3 = 708.75 ft3

708.75 ft3 × 100 lbs. per ft3 = 70,875 lbs

70,875 lbs ÷ 2,000 lbs per ton = ≈35.5 tons of sand

LIQUID CONVERSION CHART

	teaspoon	tablespoon	fluid ounce	gill	cup	pint	quart	gallon
1 teaspoon =	1	1/3	1/6	1/24	- - -	- - -	- - -	- - -
1 tablespoon =	3	1	1/2	1/8	1/16	- - -	- - -	- - -
1 fluid ounce =	6	2	1	1/4	1/8	1/16	- - -	- - -
1 gill =	24	8	4	1	1/2	1/4	1/8	- - -
1 cup =	48	16	8	2	1	1/2	1/4	1/16
1 pint =	96	32	16	4	2	1	1/2	1/8
1 quart =	192	64	32	8	4	2	1	1/4
1 gallon =	768	256	128	32	16	8	4	1
1 firkin =	6912	2304	1152	288	144	72	36	9
1 hogshead =	48384	16128	8064	2016	1008	504	252	63

DRY WEIGHT MEASUREMENT CHART

Dry Weight Measurements

		Ounces	Pounds	Metric
1/16 teaspoon	a dash			
1/8 teaspoon or less	a pinch or 6 drops			.5 ml
1/4 teaspoon	15 drops			1 ml
1/2 teaspoon	30 drops			2 ml
1 teaspoon	1/3 tablespoon	1/6 ounce		5 ml
3 teaspoons	1 tablespoon	1/2 ounce		14 grams
1 tablespoon	3 teaspoons	1/2 ounce		14 grams
2 tablespoons	1/8 cup	1 ounce		28 grams
4 tablespoons	1/4 cup	2 ounces		56.7 grams
5 tablespoons plus 1 teaspoon	1/3 cup	2.6 ounces		75.6 grams
8 tablespoons	1/2 cup	4 ounces	1/4 pound	113.4 grams
10 tablespoons plus 2 teaspoons	2/3 cup	5.2 ounces		158 ml
12 tablespoons	3/4 cup	6 ounces	.375 pound	177 ml
16 tablespoons	1 cup	8 ounces	1/2 pound	225 ml
32 tablespoons	2 cups	16 ounces	1 pound	450 ml
64 tablespoons	4 cups or 1 quart	32 ounces	2 pounds	907 ml

$$\text{GPM (per nozzle)} = \frac{\text{GPA} \times \text{MPH} \times \text{W}}{5{,}940}$$

$$\text{GPM (per nozzle)} = \frac{\text{Gallons per 1,000 sq ft} \times \text{MPH} \times \text{W}}{136}$$

$$\text{GPM (per nozzle)} = \frac{\text{Ounces collected} \times 60}{\text{Collection Time} \times 128}$$

$$\text{GPA} = \frac{\text{GPM (per nozzle)} \times 5{,}940}{\text{MPH} \times \text{W}}$$

$$\text{Gallons per 1,000 sq ft} = \frac{\text{GPM (per nozzle)} \times 136}{\text{MPH} \times \text{W}}$$

$$\text{GPM} = \frac{\text{OPM}}{128}$$

Percentage Mixing: To determine the amount of pesticide needed to make a solution (or suspension) containing a certain percentage of the active ingredient (a.i.), use one of the following formulas:

For **emulsifiable concentrates** and other liquid formulations–

$$\text{No. of gal. needed} = \frac{\text{gal. of spray wanted} \times \% \text{ a.i. wanted} \times 8.345 \text{ (lbs. per gal.)}}{\text{lbs. a.i. per gal. of concentrate} \times 100}$$

For **wettable powder** formulations–

$$\text{No. of lbs. needed} = \frac{\text{gal. of spray wanted} \times \% \text{ a.i. wanted} \times 8.345 \text{ (lbs. per gal.)}}{\% \text{ a.i. in pesticide used}}$$

Speed	Time required in seconds to cover course distance		
MPH	**100 ft**	**200 ft**	**300 ft**
1.0	68	136	205
1.5	45	91	136
2.0	34	68	102
2.5	27	54	81
3.0	23	45	68
3.5	20	39	58
4.0	17	34	51
4.5	15	30	45
5.0	14	27	41
5.5	x	25	37
6.0	x	23	34
6.5	x	21	31
7.0	x	19	29
7.5	x	18	27
8.0	x	17	26
8.5	x	16	24
9.0	x	15	23

x = not recommended

$$\text{MPH} = \frac{\text{Distance (ft)} \times 60}{\text{Time (seconds)} \times 88}$$

COMMON CONVERSION FACTORS

Multiply…	**by…**	**to get…**
Acres	43,560	Square feet
	4,840	Square yards
	4,047	Square meters
	0.4047	Hectares
Centimeters	0.394	Inches
	0.0328	Feet
	0.01	Meters
	10	Millimeters
Cubic centimeters	0.06102	Cubic inches
	1	Milliliter
Cubic inches	16.39	Cubic centimeters
Cup	0.5	Pints
	8	Fluid ounces
	16	Tablespoons
Feet	12	Inches
	304.8	Millimeters
	30.48	Centimeters
	0.3048	Meters
Gallons	4	Quarts
	8	Pints
	16	Cups
	128	Fluid ounces
	231	Cubic inches
	3,785	Milliliters
	3.785	Liters

Gallons of water	8.3453	Pounds of water
	3.785	Kilograms of water
Gallons per acre	2.47	Gallons per hectare
	9.35	Liters per hectare
Multiply…	**by…**	**to get…**
Grams	0.03527	Fluid ounces
	1,000	Milligrams
	0.001	Kilograms
Hectares	2.47	Acres
	107,639	Square feet
	10,000	Square meters
Inches	25.4	Millimeters
	2.54	Centimeters
Kilograms	1,000	Grams
	35.274	Ounces (dry)
	2.205	Pounds
Kilograms per hectare	0.89	Pounds per acre
Kilometers	3,280.8	Feet
	1,093.6	Yards
	0.6214	Miles
	1,000	Meters
Liters	1,000	Milliliters
	33.8	Fluid ounces
	61.02	Cubic inches
	2.113	Pints
	1.057	Quarts

	0.264	Gallons
Meters	39.37	Inches
	3.281	Feet
	1.094	Yards
	100	Centimeters
	0.001	Kilometers
	1,000	Millimeters
Miles	1,760	Yards
	5,280	Feet
	1,609	Meters
	1.609	Kilometers
Multiply…	**by…**	**to get…**
Miles per hour	88	Feet per minute
	1.609	Kilometers per hour
Milliliters	0.0338	Fluid ounces
	0.06	Cubic inches
	1	Cubic centimeter
Millimeters	0.0394	Inches
	0.1	Centimeters
Ounces (dry)	0.0625	Pounds
	28.35	Grams
Ounces (liquid)	0.125	Cups
	2	Tablespoons
	6	Teaspoons
	0.0078125	Gallons
	29.57	Milliliters

Multiply...	by...	to get...
	0.02957	Liters
Parts per million	0.0001	Percent (%)
	1	Milligram per liter
	1	Milligram per kilogram
Percent (%)	10,000	Parts per million
Pints (liquid)	2	Cups
	16	Fluid ounces
	0.125	Gallons
	473	Milliliters
	0.473	Liters
Pounds	16	Ounces
	453.6	Grams
	0.4536	Kilograms
Pounds per acre	1.12	Kilograms per hectare
Quarts (liquid)	2	Pints
	4	Cups
	32	Fluid ounces
	946	Milliliters
	0.946	Liters
Multiply...	**by...**	**to get...**
Square centimeters	0.155	Square inches
Square feet	144	Square inches
	929	Square centimeters
	0.0000229	Acres
	0.00000929	Hectares
Square inches	0.007	Square feet

	6.45	Square centimeters
Square kilometers	247.1	Acres
	0.386	Square miles
	100	Hectares
Square meters	1,550	Square inches
	10.76	Square feet
	1.196	Square yards
Square miles	640	Acres
	259	Hectares
Square yards	1,296	Square inches
	9	Square feet
	8,361	Square centimeters
	0.8361	Square meters
Tablespoons	0.5	Fluid ounces
	3	Teaspoons
	0.0625	Cups
	14.8	Milliliters
Teaspoons	0.17	Fluid ounces
	4.9	Milliliters
Ton (US)	2,000	Pounds
	907.2	Kilograms
Ton (metric)	2,204.6	Pounds
	1,000	Kilograms
Yards	3	Feet
	36	Inches
	0.914	Meters

1 acre-inch of water = 27,154.2 gal

1 inch of water per 1,000 sq ft = 623.4 gal

1 milliliter or cubic centimeter of water weighs 1 gram

1 liter of water weighs 1 kilogram

1 gallon of water weighs 8.3453 pounds

1 gallon of water weighs 3.785 kilograms

To calculate the surface area of a pond, mark a rectangle around the pond with lines A-C and B-D equal in length and touching the ends of the pond. Measure offset lines at regular intervals from the rectangle base lines to the edge of the pond. In this example, the offset lines are 10 feet apart. Add the two offset distances at each interval as shown in the following example.

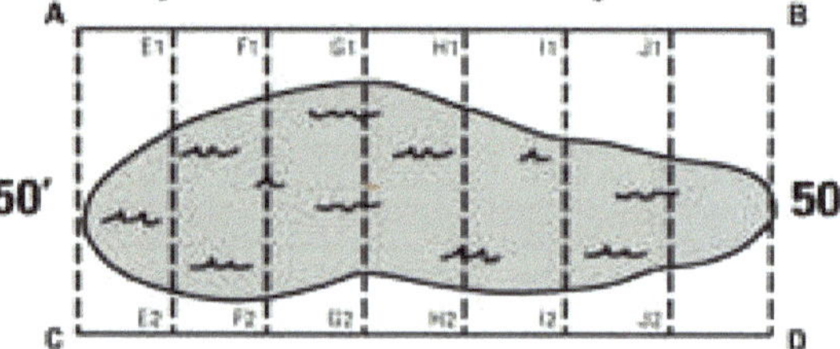

E1 = 15 ft	F1 = 7 ft	= 6 ft	H1 = 11 ft
E2 = 6 ft	F2 = 4 ft	= 7 ft	H2 = 4 ft
= 21 ft	= 11 ft	= 13 ft	= 15 ft

I1 = 15 ft	J1 = 18 ft
I2 = 4 ft	J2 = 7 ft
= 19 ft	= 25 ft

Subtract each of these offset line totals from the distance between A and C (in this case 50 ft) to find the width of the pond at the 10-foot intervals.

A-C distance		Line set Totals		Offset Length
50 ft	-	21 ft	=	29 ft
50 ft	-	11 ft	=	39 ft
50 ft	-	13 ft	=	37 ft
50 ft	-	15 ft	=	35 ft
50 ft	-	19 ft	=	31 ft
50 ft	-	25 ft	=	25 ft
				196 ft

Multiply the offset total by the distance between offset lines to find the surface area of the pond:

196 ft x 10 ft = 1,960 sq. ft.

TEMPERATURE CONVERSION:

To convert Celsius (ºC) to Fahrenheit (ºF): multiply by 1.8 and add 32

To convert Fahrenheit (ºF) to Celsius (ºC): subtract 32 and multiply by 0.56

Temperature Conversion

°C	°F
100	212
95	203
90	194
80	185
75	176
70	160
65	150
60	140
55	130
50	122
45	113
40	104
35	95
30	86
25	77
20	68
15	60
10	50
5	41
0	32
-5	29
-10	14
-15	5
-20	-4

-25   -13
-30   -22
-35   -31
-40   -40